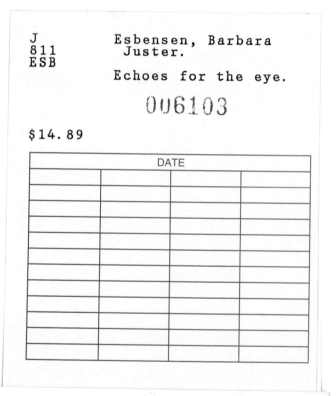

Echoes for the Eye

Poems to Celebrate Patterns in Nature

by Barbara Juster Esbensen

illustrated by Helen K. Davie

HarperCollins*Publishers*

For Helen K. Davie because we dreamed this book.
Once again you have read my words and painted
their shapes with your magic brush. Thank you.
—B.J.E.

To all the exceptional people who challenge us to
fully use our minds and our senses to reveal
and cherish the wonders of our world
—H.K.D.

ECHOES FOR THE EYE
Poems to Celebrate Patterns in Nature
Text copyright © 1996 by Barbara Juster Esbensen
Illustrations copyright © 1996 by Helen K. Davie
Printed in the United States of America. For information address
HarperCollins Children's Books, a division of HarperCollins Publishers,
10 East 53rd Street, New York, NY 10022.

Library of Congress Cataloging-in-Publication Data
Esbensen, Barbara Juster.
  Echoes for the eye : poems to celebrate patterns in nature/ by Barbara Juster
Esbensen ; illustrated by Helen K. Davie.
    p.   cm.
  Summary: A collection of poems that reveal patterns in nature.
  ISBN 0-06-024398-8. — ISBN 0-06-024399-6 (lib. bdg.)
  1. Shape—Juvenile poetry.   2. Nature—Juvenile poetry.   3. Children's
poetry, American. [1. Shape—Poetry.   2. Nature—Poetry.   3. American
poetry.] I. Davie, Helen, ill. II. Title.
PS3555.S24E83   1996   94-623
811'.54—dc20   CIP
                                                                          AC

Typography by Elynn Cohen
1 2 3 4 5 6 7 8 9 10
❖
First Edition

Contents

A Note from the Author

A kind of natural geometry and a repetition of shapes exist in unexpected places in the world around us. Living things found in the seas, under the earth, and in the meadows, deserts, and forests of our planet imitate one another.

Lightning and your veins have something in common. Hailstones bouncing on the roof mimic objects in the darkness of space.

In the Middle Ages, a mathematician named Leonardo Fibonacci developed a number pattern that has been given his name: the Fibonacci series. By starting with 1, 1 and always adding the two previous numbers together, we get the next one. The Fibonacci series looks like this: 1, 1, 2, 3, 5, 8, 13, 21, 34, 55, 89, 144 and on and on.

and the Illustrator

Fibonacci counted many things in nature. When he counted the spiral rows in pinecones and pineapples and daisies, he noticed that they were always numbers that appeared in his series. If you count the spiral rows of seeds in most sunflowers, you will get 55 growing in one direction and 89 spiraling in the opposite direction. Try it and see!

We have both spent most of our lives noticing, learning about, and marveling at these patterns in the natural world, and in the universe that holds our planet Earth.

We hope that our book will open your eyes to the mystery and the beauty of these repeating forms.

Barbara J. Eckersen

Helen K. Davie

Spirals

Every spring,
lifting out of the damp earth,
ferns
like coiled green wires
push up through leafmold
into the new sun
Spiral shapes wound tight
curled underground
all winter
unwind
like green
mainsprings inside the earth's
dark clock

In summer gardens
sunflowers
hold
yellow faces
to the sky
their stiff-crowned seeds
hardpacked
in flying spirals
curving
clockwise and counter-
clockwise   Count
the whirling 55   the
dizzy spinning 89 —
the rows and
rows of old Italian
arithmetic!

Watch out!   Hurricane coming!
Living mountains of black water
lift out of the sea
and race for the continent's
fragile edge

High in some empty place
warm and cold collide
and spin
their terrible
winds
around a moving
unblinking
eye

Tornado warning!
Fierce
spiraling
columns of air
speed across the land
twist
out of heavy black storm clouds
out of the sick green-lit
sky
Air
brainless
blind
air
gone wild!

*H*idden
in your head
in your own ear
a spiral receiver
of every sound
every
whisper   every bark
whine
whinny
mew
musical note
beat
of every drum
someone calling
your name
every
siren   every cry
laugh
shout
cheer
winds down into your ear
Call it
cochlea!

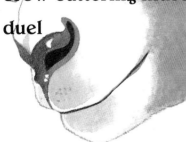

Precarious
on the rocky slopes
bighorn sheep
slam head against
head
each strong horn
a boney helix
curling out   curling
out
from every heavy
skull

Mountains ring
with the clatter
and clash   with
the head-cracking
brow-battering muscular
duel

*E*very year
silently growing
beneath the sea
the nautilus shell
adds
a pearl-glazed room

Each locked chamber
smooth-walled
larger than the one before

No furniture   no
lights
only
the sheen of pearl
only the curved
ceilings
uncoiling
one by one   every
year under the tossing
sea

Uncounted galaxies
send their silver light
unwinding
into
the blackness of space

Above our heads in the night sky
stretches
the Milky Way —
a starry roadway   a pinwheel
of stars   a
spiral of dusty light

Our glowing blue planet
floats in the arms
whirling out
from the galaxy's center
millions of miles away

Branches

Against the blowing sky
the stiff
fabric of branches and twigs
grows up and
up into the light

Spreading
unseen beneath the tree
a tangle of roots —
secret fingers
that feel their way
through the unmapped
country
underground

Veins
thread their thin
pattern
through every leaf   Look
how they hold each green
hand
open to the sun
collecting light and the green
diamond-drops of water!

In the instant before thunder
lightning
streaks from the dark sky
to the ground
It leaps
like jagged fire from cloud to cloud
sends out its sizzling
electric branches

The bright electric charge
crackles
The stunning energy
grows and spreads
like a fierce electric
tree
in the wild stormy air

$\mathcal{V}$eins
thread their thin paths
their narrow blue
roadways under
your skin

All
of your body's
blood
all the   busy traffic
— the coming and the
going
of its chemistry —
flows and branches and
branches again
like an echo
of the oak tree's leafless
silhouette
against the blowing sky

Polygons

Honeybee!   Yes
you!   You in the black
and yellow
suit
lend me your
ruler   your
protractor
I must measure these
honeyed angles
these sweet storage
bins
these
closepacked waxy rooms

Fly away
honeybee
Do not watch me
break
the manysided
lock   Do not see me
steal
this
nectar-jam
dripping golden from
my tongue!

No twin shapes
sparkle here   No
crystalline clones
drift and settle
and fill
our deepening boot
tracks   Each
flake carefully cut
its six points
precise   Every
frosty star
unique   Who
performs such
twinkling
lapidary magic?

Under cool rocking water
where the turtle swims
skeins of sunlight
waver on the sand

Shifting patterns   nets of
light
trace the fitted
geometric tiles —
finished jigsaw puzzle
(not a piece missing!)
on the turtle's shell

Climbing the hot bank
the turtle
hauls a wet smear
across
the dry geometry
across
the cracking angled lines
lightly rulered in the
mud

Meanders

Bull snake   rattle
snake
cottonmouth
sliding through grass
whipping
your way along the water

Show me how you
loop your scales
how you slide your
S-curves
scribbling no word
and   with a hiss
dis-
appearing!

Pouring over rocks
braiding and unbraiding
pushing against each bank
flattening itself into
satin curves
the shining river
cuts its snake-way
across the flowered land

Like a frozen white river
locked in time
the glacier
slides
slow
ponderous
inch by heavy
inch
powerful
grinding —
a heavy unfolding
ribbon of snow and ice

Circles

Did you see?   Did you
see
the rainbow-scaled fish
arch into the air
and fall?

Did you see
those perfect circles?
Those hoops of water and light?
They fit together   one
inside another

Wider and wider
they grow
out
and
out
and   out
from the quick splash
to the shore

Circles
set in wood — concentric
a round calendar
Its widening rings grow slowly
out
 and out
 and   out
from the old tree's
earliest day
to the shore of
now

A circle
is the shape of
safety where wolf
shadows
prowl in the far north
where
musk oxen stand — spokes
of a dark muscular
wheel

Their massive heads
point in every direction
a watchful compass-rose
set in the snow

Deep in the forest
curled in its grassy
bed
the fawn
lies
dappled with circles
lies
hidden under
medallions of sunlight
and woodland gloom
almost invisible

Think of a circle think
of our planet
Earth
solid globe
spinning holding us
holding
oceans and forests and drifting
deserts
in the blackness of space

Think of the sun
our blazing disk our
daystar
and the planet spinning from
day into night and
return
Think of all that light
washing over us
flowing into starlit dark —
A whirling cycle of days
and nights

A circle
is the shape of sleep
In hollow places
deep under winter snow
small animals dream   Their toes
are tucked up
their tails curl down
and around

Heavy circular bears
breathe
the slow sleep of cold
nights and days

31

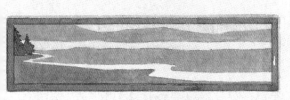

Sleep draws a soft line around you
curled and folded
in the arc of an arm
holding the nighttime book

At the foot of the bed
the orange and white cat
has wound herself tight
and the circle of moon coming in
fits her shape exactly

Echoes for the eye!